T0077886

Moments of J.O.Y.

VOLUME ONE

ANGEL HINMAN

WESTBOW PRESS®
PRESS®
A DIVISION OF THOMAS NELSON
& ZONDERVAN

WestBow Press books may be ordered through booksellers or by contacting:

WestBow Press
A Division of Thomas Nelson & Zondervan
1663 Liberty Drive
Bloomington, IN 47403
www.westbowpress.com
1 (866) 928-1240

ISBN: 978-1-9736-0472-3 (sc)
ISBN: 978-1-9736-0473-0 (hc)
ISBN: 978-1-9736-0471-6 (e)

Library of Congress Control Number: 2017915726

Print information available on the last page.

WestBow Press rev. date: 11/09/2017

To my heart in three, that smells like mud puddles
and peanut butter. Y'all bring me so much *joy!*

Preface

On a blustery Christmas Eve, my little family gathered into a crowded candle light service to hear our pastor friend give a message on living a life with true joy. He shared that the J.O.Y. life was one spent living for Jesus first, others second, and yourself last. Such a simple premise for true joy leapt at me, especially as it echoed Jesus' teachings. I felt called to begin a small devotional site, sharing things I read in my quiet time with friends that were unchurched or in the same place of life as myself.

Creating the J.O.Y. Life has been an adventure with God and I couldn't be more grateful for my community; my family, friends and neighbors that have contributed to help make it what it has become and continues to morph into.

As I decided to write a devotional, I wanted to leave room for thought. This little book has margins for you to fill with your own thoughts and impressions. Please write in this book! I promise that it will give you great joy to look back and read about where you have come from later in life. Documenting our walk with God, the miracles he has performed in our own lives and the trials he has carried us through, should be as important as documenting our lives on social media. Even more so, actually. So fill those spaces up!

Going through this devotional, I also encourage you to look up the scriptures. God's word makes my impressions meager; so go straight to the source for all truth, hope and joy! If you don't have a Bible, get ahold of me, and I will gladly get one into your hands. And, as always, if you have any questions, comments or stories of true joy, I want to hear them! Please, email me at angel.hinman@gmail.com!

May God's joy follow you as you embark on this devotional journey, and may the J.O.Y. Life transform your outlook on how you live.

Joyfully,
Angel

Heaven is Our Joy

When one of my oldest and dearest friends went into labor recently, I found myself consumed with anticipation. As I prayed for her and her sweet babe, I had butterflies in my stomach! The level of excitement I felt took me by surprise. I realized that the older I get, the tougher it can be to find true thrills in this life.

Long days, longer nights, work, financial pressures, relationships, communication and consistent global crisis wear me down. It's important to be reminded that we are allowed to get excited, and in a spiritual sense we are called to an anticipation of Christ and Heaven. Which is why, no matter what, I think it is crucial to live everyday focused on the prize of heaven and eternal life with Christ.

Sure, it's easy to say to anyone, "Focus on the prize, not the work" but when you are in the grueling training for that prize, it can look and feel pretty bleak, can't it!?

What can help is staying fully engaged in the relationships and moments around us, remembering that each moment we are passing through is one that brings us closer to Him and His presence. Jump headfirst into your life, Friend! Jesus, others, you; the J.O.Y life.

Romans 8:18, Micah 7:7

Dear Heavenly Father, I know that one day, I too will be a heavenly being! To consider an eternity without pain, suffering, aches; Oh Father! I cannot even fathom Your greatness and love. Thank you that You have given me this day to live through, despite the challenges and struggles I will face. Give me a vision for Your will in my life and help me to stay focused on that today. I love you, Lord! For all of these things I pray in Jesus' name. Amen.

ℛemain Faithful

Recently, I was grumbling to myself because my kids wouldn't go to sleep. Suddenly, I recalled an event that took place while I had been out with a friend at a playground. Directly in front of me a little boy had fallen down and began to cry, calling for his mother. His grandmother came over, and rather than comfort him, she said, "You shush. You know your Momma isn't coming to take care of you, she never has before, and she's not going to start today. Now get up and get on or we are leaving." No judgments are being made here towards that grandmother, but the look on that child's face was utter shame and heartache. Her words crushed him, and crumpled my heart into a trash can ready wad. What does this have to do with faith? Folks, if we are faithful to our efforts, even when it feels impossible because we are exhausted and cranky, tired and fed up, overwhelmed and miserable, there will be others around us that won't have that look of pain cross their face. There will be healthy friends, family members, and children. Strength and peace come from our efforts of faithfulness. The "O" in J.O.Y. life stands for "others." Let's make our faith a bridge to others around us. Faithfulness is a gift we can give each day!

John 7:38

Dear God, you are so perfect Father! I marvel at Your perfection, and I feel my flaws today. Thank You for sending Jesus to give an example of the depth of Your goodness. Please help me with my frustration, anger, sadness, and apathy. Take away my lack of patience. Restore to me the full measure of faith that I need to pursue You and Your will for my life, instead of my own missions. And Father, please protect my joy. Keep it safe from the enemy, in Jesus name I pray. Amen

Strength and peace come from our efforts of faithfulness.

Can You Trust Him?

I have friends that are democrats and republicans. I have friends that are men and women, black and white and brown, straight and gay. They are all very different, beautiful and I love them *all* very much. My faith in Jesus' love for them is far stronger than any different opinions I might have about their life choices or sins. I have faith that Jesus has room in His kingdom for all of them, and my prayer today and every day is that my faith is alive enough, active enough, and honest enough to see this materialize. Can you trust Him enough to let the differences, pain, frustrations and hurts go? He can handle it, I promise! Then you will be free to love Him and others.

Psalm 55:22

Dear Father, can You see all this sin? It is all around me, and often in me. Please forgive me, Father, for the sins I have committed. Help me to see my sin and to stop judging others while I sit in a place of spiritual failure. Thank you for Your generous love. Fill me up with this never ending, never failing, never giving up love so that I might be able to pour it out on my loved ones and those that You have called me to. I love you Father! For all these things I pray in Your mighty name Jesus. Amen.

Who is He Building in Us?

When I look in the mirror I see a girl-woman who needs her eye brows plucked, has a stubborn last few post-baby pounds to lose, hair that needs a trim and way too many freckles for someone approaching their thirties. She's a generally brave and goofy gal, who loves people, eats new foods as often as possible, and is too curious for her own good.

Each year on my birthday I take time to look at myself in the mirror. Normally I am so helter skelter that a quick glance is all that I get. And while I think this practice could be misconstrued as vain, I look at this practice as a means to really see who I am: To remember where I got that scar. To recall why it's okay that things have changed. It's a chance to consider all the people and places that God has brought me since last year.

While it's important, crucial even, to know ourselves; it must be in context of God's greater picture. Who is He building in us, what is our purpose? What is our why?

1Thessalonians 5:5

Father, You are so beyond my comprehension. I can not understand why I am here at times, but I trust Your plan for me. Can You show me today where to go, who to reach out to, how to act, what to say? Lead me each day Father. Let me see You in me, when I look in the mirror. For all these things I pray in Your mighty name Jesus. Amen

$\mathcal{L}$etter to the Lord

Gifts are great, but for a girl who loves the written word, cards are the sustenance of the soul. When I get the mail and I find a note written by a friend, I always smile. I always feel loved. I always feel like I have meaning.

The single, most powerful growth tool that I have used on my faith walk, after the Bible, is the concept of a note to God. I write God dozens of notes a year, telling Him what I see in Him, how my life is going, and where I need Him the most. These letters have grown my faith in Him, and I believe that, in part, they help me to put into words the true God I know, not just some superficial reflection of what God could look like.

God is my best friend, and I want Him to feel the same joy that I grab ahold of when I get letters in the mail! While I don't post the notes, I form them in a prayer, and God has promises that He hears us, always. Can you build your relationship with Christ in this manner today?

Psalm 145:18

J.O.Y. Life Challenge:

Take the time to write a letter to God! And while you are at it, send one to a friend who has influenced your life!

No Doubt

While considering faith, the most obvious opponent our belief is doubt. Doubt keeps us from moving forward in faith. It keeps us from going forward in relationships. Most of all, it keeps us from walking where God would have us go. I have been a part of a small project for a little over a year, and it is time consuming. I get paid very little for my efforts, but just this weekend, I found out about a big opportunity that might come from being faithful to this at times trying project. My doubts have poured in, but in my gut, I knew I needed to keep up my efforts. I am excited to see where this goes, and blessed to see faith in action.

I am certain that this situation in one of a billion in God's kingdom. He has places that He plans to take you due to your faithfulness. The things that we feel the most strongly for, doubts or no, can have the biggest gains on the other end. Be full of faith today, Friend!

James 1:6

God, there are so many opponents to my faith. Please take my faith to a place where my doubts fall away, one by one. Give me strength to see the power and might that You have shown and possess. Help me to lean into this strength and trust You to carry me through this difficult place of doubt. I thank you for Your victory and for the rewards You promise me for my faith! I love you God, and I trust You today. For all these things I pray in Your mighty name Jesus. Amen.

Doubt keeps us from moving forward in faith.

Full of Faith

Faith is a verb, an action word. It calls us to take part in something. It moves us. America needs less verbiage and a whole lot more verbs. When I woke up today, my plan was to rest, and to not leave my house. Then I heard about five police officers who were killed in a Dallas shooting.

My heart was already so heavy from the horrors of the week, so of course I sobbed. The big, blubbering, crying mess that I was decided not to let another day go by feeling inept. I loaded the kids up, and we took lunch to local law enforcement officers and their families. We are not sitting still. We will be faithful. People full of faith; we can not lose because Christ has already won.

Today, people need the living Christ that is in you. They need you to carry that light into their darkness. Can you take a meal? Make a phone call and give an encouraging word? How can you, being full of faith, impact God's kingdom today, Friend?

Romans 15:13

Father God, open my eyes. Show me just a glimpse of the heart ache that is all around me. Help me not to live blindly, but to be aware of the pain that the Enemy is creating everywhere. And God, today remind me of the power my faith in You contains. Give me the energy, desire and tenacity to follow You where You send me. Help me to help others today, Lord. Help me to carry out my faith in action. Thank you Lord for never leaving me, especially when I am in the toughest places. I love you Father! For all these things I pray in Your mighty name Jesus. Amen

Faith is a verb, an action word. It calls us to take part in something. It moves us.

Faith and Trust

I want to be a "faithful" wife. My greatest hope and prayer is to raise my sons to have a living "faith." If the word "faith" had a soul mate, it'd be the word "trust." They belong together, by definition, and this is why it is such a challenge to have faith.

As humans, we have been hurt and jaded enough times to find trust leaves a bad taste in our mouths. But we must trust in the Lord and take a step of faith. God has not given us a life to be spent calculating risk or being careful. He gave us minds to think. Bodies to push. Spirits to express. Souls to nurture. We can trust in Him and His plan and have faith that He will carry us through whatever we face with a faithfulness that is utterly perfect.

There is no need for fear today Friend. Trust in God, for He will be faithful to you, in every way and in every place, at all times. Forever.

John 11:25-26, 1 John 5:4

God, please help me to let go of my distrust. First, bring my heart the strength to forgive those who have violated my trust. Help me let go of my pain and my hurt from those moments. Lord, lend me Your eyes, that I might see the many ways that You have already proven Your faithfulness to me. Remind me, Father of Your perfect track record, that I might recall all the moments that You were there for me and carried me through. Thank you Father for those times! Thank you that You will carry me today just as You did then! I love you Father! For all these things I pray in Your mighty name Jesus. Amen.

If the word "faith" had a soul mate, it'd be the word "trust."

It's Okay

It's okay. It's okay if you aren't particularly happy-hearted today. If your life seems full of things to be thankful for, yet you still find yourself sad, lonely, longing, or even depressed, it's okay.

When the pilgrims sat with their "friends" the Native Americans for the first Thanksgiving, they had all lost loved ones. They had all experienced sickness, persecution, anger, frustration, poverty, hunger, disease and inhuman treatment either first or second hand. But they sat. They broke bread. They gave thanks. Thank God for what you can, and ask Him to bear the burden of whatever you can't today! Take lots of deep breaths my friends, because He's got it, and He will take care of it!

Psalm 95:2-3, 2 Corinthians 4:15-16

J.O.Y. Life Challenge:

I know singing isn't everyone's cup of tea. It's certainly not mine. But there is something so powerful in worshipping the Lord with song. You need a praise song, Friend. Find one song that is specially yours. It needs to be a song that stirs your heart, gets your blood pumping for the Lord, and opens your spirit in a way that ushers in a time of thanksgiving. Find that song. And then play it, regularly. Praise Him with your songs, and watch as amazing things begin to unfold in your life.

Roots of Faith

What do you believe in? Faith begins by answering this question.

When we face truth that we can stand on, our faith takes root. I was out driving late into the night with my husband recently. We were speaking about God and our lives. My birthday is coming up soon and I shared with my husband that as a youth, I never thought about myself as any older than I am right now. The thought of living past this age is one big conundrum, not because I never thought I'd make it to here or anything dramatic like that. I just never considered life after 27! Funny huh?

But we both agreed that God had a much grander plan for our lives than the one we might have chosen or imagined. I believe in God's plan for my life. I have faith that He knows what is best for me. I want to be faithful (full of faith) to that belief. And you know what? I think being a person of faith brings unseen joy to my life.

Hebrews 12:2

God, I believe in You. I trust that You sent Your Son to die on the cross for me. I believe that after living a perfect life He was killed and rose again after three days. I believe that He is my Savior. Father, I also trust that You created me for a reason. I am here for Your will to be fulfilled, and I am grateful to be a part of Your plan, Father! Help me today to be full of faith in You and Your perfect plan! I love you Father! For all these things I pray in Your mighty name Jesus. Amen.

Laugh With the Lord

We hear people say "God has a funny sense of humor," all the time. I would have to agree wholeheartedly. I dearly love to laugh, and grew up in a home where there was plenty of teasing and joking. My dad in particular was always fond of a good prank or joke. We went to eat earlier this year, just he and me and my brand new baby, and he said, "Angel, I really am glad you are such a goof ball. It's made my life a lot better." And I could have said the exact same thing to him.

Life hurts, you know? It's hard and exhausting and everything in the world is causing cancer and wild animals are trying to eat kids and...Oh. My. Word. We have to laugh. We have to find solidarity through mirth. Because crying might be the only alternative. Laugh today friends. Pull a (harmless) prank. Tell a joke. And look out for God's little snippets of humor too!

Psalm 37:13, Psalm 2:4

Wow God! This life is full to bursting with moments that are silly and ridiculous. Help me to laugh with You, instead of crying. Help me to face my stress today with a smile. Show me moments of true joy and adorn my face with a smile that shines brightly of Your love and peace. Thank you for my cheeks which can actually get sore from smiling, and help me to experience that today, if it is in Your will. I love you so, Father. For all these things I pray in Your mighty name Jesus. Amen!

We have to find solidarity through mirth. Because crying might be the only alternative.

Release

My dad is one of the hardest working people I know. His work ethic has had a profound influence on my life. I love the feeling of putting in a full day's work and the reward of seeing progress made. As a youth, however, I often resented the work load that my Dad took on. I wished more than anything that he would take more time to rest, to hang out and to play. But now, as a parent of three small children, I get it. I need to work almost constantly, just to keep my head above water. And guess what? My dad (and mom) have in recent years started to rest!

What's the point here?

It's funny how our life cycles have similar patterns. My dad makes sure to let me know that the exhaustion will ease up in many regards as my kids get older and as I mature. God does send rest to the weary, and no matter how tired we feel we can rest on Him, who is strong enough to carry our burdens.

Are you tired? Overworked? Stressed out? Let God know today. Give Him the heavy loads you carry around, and take on His rest, peace and joy!

Ephesians 3:16-17

Dear God, Today I want to thank you for the people You placed in my life to teach me powerful lessons. Without their guidance I would not be the person I am, and I am so grateful for Your faithfulness to them and to me through them. Today, I am weary. My body, mind and spirit cry out for strength and energy for the mountains of challenges I am facing. Please, Father, carry me through. Take away my bone weariness and replace it with Your awesome peace, hope and love. Thank you Father! For all these things I pray in Your mighty name Jesus. Amen.

*Give Him the heavy loads
you carry around, and take
on His rest, peace and joy!*

Super...No More

My older sons love superheroes. Who doesn't, really? We can be so attracted to the heroic and mighty, often forgetting how unrealistic and unreasonable their whole show of superiority is. Being a human is HARD. Finding balance takes great effort, self-regulation, patience, time, and a willingness to be flexible. Whether you are looking at superheroes of the comic book variety or the elite class of human that seems to have pulled it all together, remember that realistically, we are all on a balance beam together, trying not to get knocked off!

Our job is not to attack life with the intention of perfection, or even to fight the bad guys. Simply put, it's our role to be the light of the world. To bring forth joy, peace, hope, laughter, kindness and the fruits of the spirit.

Don't try too hard today; just do your very best with God to illuminate the darkness that surrounds us. That's enough. We must remember that He has already defeated the enemy!

Matthew 5:14-16, Galatians 5:22

J.O.Y. Life Challenge:

Four Ideas to Illuminate the World:

1. Start a pay it forward when you buy your coffee today. Pay for the person in line behind you, and remember to pray for that person!

2. Flip through your contacts in your phone/social media/ email/phone book and send an encouraging message to someone. Remember to pray for them as well!
3. Compliment a stranger.
4. Get food for someone; nothing brings an opportunity to shine like offering food!

$\mathcal{B}$alance in the Trinity

The people who are closest to us have a lot of insight into our needs, strengths and weaknesses. God placed these specific "others" in our lives because they will be strong where we are not. They will balance us. They can and will help us. I think of the Trinity as the perfect example. There is the Father, the son, and the Holy Spirit. Just like an egg has a shell, the egg white and the yolk; God is one entity in three parts. The right amount of all three make an egg, and the same goes for God. Balance is in God's DNA. He wants it for us as well. I think a good place to start is getting to know His three parts.

The Father, Holy God, is all powerful and mighty. He is the great creator, the judge, the strength that we can turn to for all of our needs. Jesus, our teacher, giver of eternal life, and living sacrifice can be our role model in all situations. The Holy Spirit, wise guide, peaceful comforter and encouragement can be trusted to help us make it through the many trials we face in this life.

Ephesians 6:10, 2 Corinthians 12:9, Romans 8:5-6

Dear God, Holy One, thank you for sending the Son to Earth that I might have His example to follow all of my days. Help me to draw close to the Holy Spirit, learning to live by Him and not of my own will and desire. In all my living, lend me strength Father that I might be able to follow Jesus and listen to the wise counsel of the Spirit. For all these things I pray in Your mighty name Jesus. Amen.

Balance is in God's DNA.

Take a Break

I regularly seek times to (mostly) unplug and escape my day to day to pursue Jesus. On one such occasion, I went to the beach. I stared at the sky a lot. I absorbed the salt air. Prayers erupted from my spirit like a volcano of dialogue with the Lord. Truthfully, my writing/work life suffered while I was away. I got "behind." But it was worth it. The breakaway was worth every second of catch up. Rest and taking time to enjoy the simple pleasures of life, while praying and meditating on God's word, is something that makes work and responsibility all the more manageable. If playing hooky can help you have the energy and inspiration to push forward, take it my Friend. Get the most out of that break, and come back ready to conquer. There is balance in that.

Exodus 33:14, Luke 6:12

J.O.Y. Life Challenge:

Light a candle and wrap yourself up in your favorite blanket, sweatshirt or cool sheet, and sit/lie quietly in your favorite spot with peaceful music playing. Acknowledge God and open your heart to Him. Let Him carry your burdens away one by one, as you pour your heart out to Him. As your weights lessen, thank Him. ***Don't put a time on this exercise, Friend!

Relationship Check-Up

If Jesus expressed that our greatest responsibilities were to love Him and love others, it is fairly obvious that our relationships are the framework for our lives. People can come into our lives and completely throw us off balance. There are times when this is a gift from God, meant to bring us closer to Him. There are also times in which we feel like the intruders are an inevitable black hole, sucking us into their abyss of misery; and truly we are certain that their presence is not from God. How are your relationships today? Are they bringing you a solid foundation and supporting the beams of your ever growing life-house? Are you building others up in the way you want to be built up?

Jesus spent His entire ministry giving us a living, breathing example of what we need to do with our relationships. He took care of the sick, the hungry, and the distraught. He brought joy into the world, at the expense of His comfort and peace. He taught others truth, and He never shirked a tough moment. Most of all, He spread a message of love and life eternal.

Matthew 22:37-39, John 15:13, Hebrews 10:24-25

God, thank you for the people You have given me to be in relationship with. (Take a moment to consider all those that God has placed in your life.) Please Father; help me honor Your commandments in these relationships. I want to treat others with love, kindness and truth, but there are so many times that I struggle with this. Please help me to recall Your example, Jesus, when I come across these people and moments of challenge. Thank you, Lord of all love. For all these things I pray in Your mighty name Jesus. Amen.

Our relationships are the framework for our lives.

Whose Voice Do You Hear in the Dark?

I attended a college graduation once that left a lasting impression. A storm raged with intimidating ferocity outside, and suddenly, in the middle of a speech, the power went out. This ceremony was held in a coliseum, a huge facility, filled with thousands of people. And in the dark, I heard my dad's overprotective voice giving a long forgotten lesson in self-defense pop into my head.

"If you are ever in a crowded place, and power goes out, get to the exit. No matter what, get there fast."

I was at that exit in seconds. And though it is silly, as I sat back down after the generators kicked in and power returned, I thought about how that lesson was so deeply embedded in me. My heavenly Father has blessed me with similar impressions, and sometimes I forget them, just like I had my dad's long ago lecture. That stuff comes out when we need it. When I think about balance, I realize much of what keeps us even keeled is the power that we give to those *other* people in our lives. And to God. Whose voice is it whispering to you in your dark moments? If it is not someone who brings balance, perhaps you should replace that voice with God's perfect influence.

Deuteronomy 4:33, Hebrews 3:15

God, I know that Your word speaks to me, as do the examples of others You have placed in my life that are more spiritually mature than I am. Can You help me to have listening ears, Lord? I need Your help to hear what truth is and to remember it. Imprint on my spirit the messages that will give me hope in the future. Send words of encouragement that will not only breathe life into my weary, dark moments, but also that I might be able to share them with the other people You have placed in my life. Lord, thank you for loving me enough to send a light for the darkness in Jesus. For all these things I pray in Your mighty name Jesus. Amen.

Lean into Your Strengths

Have you taken a personality test before? Many times we think we know ourselves and yet, a simple, objective test can change our entire perspective of who we are. Gifts and character strengths we never knew we had can be revealed. Try it if you never have! Likely, you have figured out where your strengths lie. Leaning into our strengths rather than trying to perfect our weaknesses should be a goal we all strive for. How many times have you read or heard that you weren't good at something, only to go out and try to get better at that thing? I propose we do the opposite. Rather than strive to get better at something we aren't particularly gifted in, let's apply our energy to using our strengths to the furthest reaches.

When we are so intent on doing things a certain way, paying no heed to the path God has already set before our feet, we can get lost. Today, take some time to evaluate where you are standing. Is it on solid ground, atop a foundation of strength? Is that strength from the Lord? Is it from your stubbornness and foolish will power? Is it a mix of both, something lukewarm, perhaps?

Where ever you stand, He can meet you there, and He can help you to move forward in power and confidence that you haven't realized yet.

Psalm 139:5, Romans 8:28, John 15:16

J.O.Y. Life Challenge:

Take a few moments to write down your greatest spiritual strengths. If you need a list look at Romans 12:6-8, and 1 Corinthians 12:8-10. Are you using these strengths in your daily faith walk? If not, take some time to think about how you might do so today and do that thing!

*Leaning into our strengths
rather than trying to perfect
our weaknesses should be
a goal we all strive for.*

Stand

What do we do when we get thrown off balance? When the kids get sick and there is no one who can take care of them, but we had big plans? When we get rejected? When we get blindsided? It might not make sense yet, but in time, these out of balance seasons will be met with joy, peace and hope. There will be trying times but God can take you through them.

God needs us to stand, nothing more, and nothing less when we get hit hard by the storms of life. Time and again we can see in scripture that He will fight our battles for us if only we stand and let Him. Standing can be incredibly hard when we are getting hit on all sides, but it can be done, Friend! Today, if you find that life is coming down on you hard, and on all sides, just focus on standing with all you got, asking God to take care of the rest.

Ecclesiastes 3:1, Philippians 4:1, 1 Corinthians 16:13

Today, here is my prayer for you, my Friend:

Dear God, how I love Your people. My brothers and sisters who follow You are hurting today, and that gives me great pain. Father, I know that there will be seasons in our life, but this is one tough winter. Please Father; fight the sharp wind, the icy cold and the creeping darkness that is engulfing my friends. Help them to find unexplained strength as they just stand, and let Your fierce warmth light in their spirits a fire that keeps them vigilant as You fight their battles for them. Help them to see You at work today and every day, holding them with care and love as their trials become smaller and smaller as their focus grows ever on You. Thank you Mighty Savior! I love you, Lord. For all these things I pray in Your mighty name Jesus. Amen.

God needs us to stand, nothing more, and nothing less when we get hit hard by the storms of life.

First, God

My pastor spoke once on the importance of aligning our pace of life with God's pace for us. This requires a Sabbath; good old fashioned rest. It also requires planning. He mentioned that if we do not start our day with God, but rather begin it looking at other things, we may be falling into idolatry and missing an opportunity for a God-filled day. We must be intentional with our time. To this, my six year old whispered, "Momma, that's why last week was so hard. We didn't do our Bible reading first thing each day." And he was right. I accomplished a lot last week; it was a super crammed time with some great victories and moments. But it would have been so much better had I invited my kids to see God in action, rather than their old mom. Having our priorities aligned with God's purposes for us is a goal far more easily attained when we are giving Him our firsts, not our lasts.

Can you spare a few minutes for God today, at the beginning?

Matthew 6:33, Proverbs 16:3, John 3:30

Dear God, please help me today to turn to You first. Each time that a crisis arises, help me to seek Your presence. Give me the reminders I need throughout the day to slow down and invite You in. Encourage me today Father! Show me Your hands at work, as I decrease my independence let me see Your hand on my life in ever increasing measure. I love you Lord Jesus, and I thank you so much for this time we had together. For all these things I pray in Your mighty name Jesus. Amen.

$\mathcal{H}$e Will Return to You Your Desire

A few years ago I had a God encounter. I had been pouring out to God about my future, and I audibly heard God tell me to learn to Chinese. I didn't have a reason at that moment, and I still don't to this day. It can be incredibly frustrating to be called to something so challenging without a reason as to why. My brain hurts after each lesson, and the words that I am learning get jumbled up with the three years of Spanish I studied in college, making my language seem even more stunted at times.

After a particularly frustrating lesson, I walked to my mailbox to discover a blessing. My former Chinese tutor and friend had sent me a Bible that gives the English, Chinese, and Pin Yin (Pin Yin is Chinese letters/symbols translated to the English alphabet) translation. My friend sent it to me to help inspire me, and it is continuing to bring me *so much joy*. The level of joy I felt came at just the right time. I had been so discouraged facing an impossible giant that I had no way of grappling with. My inspiration had run dry, *But God*. He used my friend to rekindle the passion in me to muddle through.

Where are you struggling with inspiration? Is there a place you need God to reignite your passion for His plan? Tell Him, offer your deadness to Him and ask for new life and He will return to you your desire.

Isaiah 40:31, Isaiah 41:18

J.O.Y. Life Challenge:

There are a million and one ways to grab ahold of inspiration, but one of the quickest is to take a moment to be grateful. Look at your life, and list the things that you have to be most grateful for today. When we dwell on what is good in our life, we often are able to move beyond the cold and dreary place where passion has died.

It's All His

Tithing is touchy subject. I have a few pastor friends and they have all joked at one time or another about the annual duty to preach on the importance of tithing 10 percent, knowing it is the one Sunday everyone will be running out the doors the second the benediction comes to a close.

I get that it is uncomfortable to give such a large portion of one's stuff away. But therein lies the problem. We think of our money, our things, our problems, our life as *ours alone*. When we begin to turn over to God what is already His, we find that the action becomes easier until it is first nature. And when it is our first nature to give to God what we have, it becomes so clear that He has our blessings in His hand, ready to pour out. We just have to let go of what we think is good so that we have open hands to catch what is actually best.

Have you been holding onto things that you might be able to let go of and release into God's care? Have you ever considered tithing and what it could mean for your life?

Proverbs 3:9-10, Malachi 3:10-12

Dear Jesus, I want to believe that You can care for my financial burdens and needs out of Your abundance, but it is a hard place to have faith. Lord, You have given me so much, and I know that Your word proclaims the need for my tithe. Help me to have faith to make the sacrifices that will open up Your blessings into my life. Please, I need You to guide me in the places that I can give and give abundantly unto the others that You have placed in my life as well. Give me a generous spirit, this and every day. Thank you for Your abundant blessings on my life, and for Your goodness and provision. I love you Lord! For all these things I pray in Your mighty name Jesus. Amen.

We just have to let go of what we think is good so that we have open hands to catch what is actually best.

Yes and No

Do you know what keeps us from staying balanced? One is the inability to say "no." Sometimes we are our own worst enemy. We have to be able to protect ourselves from the exhaustion of overbooking if we want to find any semblance of balance.

Another thief of balance is saying "no" to the wrong things. If we feel out of sorts, like a part of us isn't right, often it's because we closed a door to an opportunity.

God says to keep it simple, by either saying yes or no with conviction. As adults, we must learn how to self-regulate our busyness, leaving God space to work. If we fill our schedule so full that He has no time to come in and work, and we say no to the good things He has in store for us, like rest, we should not be surprised if balance continues to evade us. Today, say "no" to some things that are unimportant time wasters. Say "yes" to God.

Matthew 5:37, Psalm 32:8

Lord God, finding balance can seem like an impossible task. How can I give things up, Lord? Please teach me to say "yes" to the right things and to reject the rest of the busyness that comes at me constantly. Teach me with Your loving kindness how to structure my time, precious God. Thank you that You have given me so much time to manage and that You have given me free will, that I might chose to let You lead me here and in every part of my life. For all these things I pray in Your mighty name Jesus. Amen.

Say "yes" to God.

Hearing God

My father was giving a sermon one Sunday and it struck me that I am intensely tuned into his voice. As a small child, I was trained to listen to him to hear what he was saying and to pay attention. Now, as an adult, I have a tough time not listening when he speaks, even if I try!

Are you that way with your parents? So trained to hear their voices that you can't help but drown everything else out when they speak? If not your parents, then your spouse, or closest friend, or kids? Whose voice is it that you are incapable of ignoring?

I want to be so in tune to God's voice that this is how I am with Him. Practicing is the only way to get there. Today, let's practice listening for God's voice. Reading His word is such a great place to begin, and building some quiet into our life each day to practice listening will surely help.

Jeremiah 33:3

J.O.Y. Life Challenge:

Find a scripture that speaks to you, and read it a few times, then take time today to be quiet. Shut off all noise making devices. Turn the lights down, and sit or lie in a place that is comfortable. Speak to God, and then give yourself some time to just listen for His voice.

$\mathcal{L}$iving in the Present

Once, my older sons spent the night at a grandparent's home. Our third son, who was only a few months old, surprised us by singling out the picture on our wall with the largest images of his older brothers' faces. He talked to the picture for close to half an hour. His precious goos and gaaas melted me, as I realized he was missing his brothers. The scene got my cogs a turnin'. Here we were my husband and I knowing that our baby needed the one on one time with us as it's a rare thing in his little life. Yet here he was, the thing that was always keeping him from getting so much attention was the one thing he really seemed to want.

Are we guilty of this? Is God removing something from our life (for a time) to enrich it? How are we responding? Are we looking back at what was and chattering away madly, missing out on what is? Let's move forward with vigor and trust, friends! This window of blessing may shut more quickly than we could imagine.

Job 17:9, Proverbs 3:5-6

Dear Jesus, it was You who came to earth and left behind Your place in perfection in order to fulfill Your destiny, for us. Thank you, Jesus, for Your incredible sacrifice and willingness to keep at God's plan for Your life until it was finished. Help us today Lord, as we are looking back and seeing so many things to grab ahold of. We want desperately to hold onto some things and inversely can't wait to get rid of other things. Please, help us today. Give us wisdom as we search for answers and send the Holy Spirit to guide our path. Thank you, sweet Jesus. For all these things I pray in Your mighty name Jesus. Amen.

*A*bigail's Protector

Recently, I led a women's Bible study on Abigail. This poor gal was married to a jerk whose name literally meant "fool." He insulted the soon to be King David most horribly, and David was not taking it sitting down. Four hundred vicious men were about to march onto Abigail's property to slaughter and pillage. While neither her husband, nor David, handled the situation well, Abigail was wise! She jumped up, offered a huge gift, presented herself as a humble servant and spoke wisely to the warrior (almost) king. And God showed His favor on Abigail. Her husband died of a heart attack (or stroke) when she told him what she had done to save their family, and David claimed her as his wife.

There are lots of jerks and hot headed people out in this world, grumbling over their lot in life. But there is also God. And He sees and knows all things, especially how we respond to those who would goad us into a battle today. Can we seek God's will as we face our challengers today?

Take some time to read the story of Abigail today. It's worth your time and bursting at the seams with action!

1 Samuel 25:1-42

J.O.Y. Life Challenge:

Take out an index card or a small sheet of paper. Think about some of the fools in your life. Who drives you crazy? Makes you angry easiest? That person who really knows how to push your buttons is the person I want you to write down on your paper. Once you've got their name down, list the ways in which Abigail dealt with her husband Nabal's foolishness that you might be able to tailor to your own "fool." Now, get to work on praying for God to change that person, and watch as your joy becomes full. Because change is going to take place.

Obedience is the Victory

Sometimes God gives us a mission. We get the job done, and then we painfully realize that the entire thing was a flop. Except for our obedience. When this happens, I have a strong suspicion that two things are going on.

First, someone else isn't being obedient. It takes two to tango, right? If you show up, do what you are supposed to with God and meet failure, the other members of the event in question may just not be in obedience. You cannot control other people. You can pray for them, and work with them as long as God has called you to, but then you must move on and understand that God is calling you to walk into new place.

Second, maybe, just maybe, the obedience was the victory and the failure we feel is not shared by God, who measures success in a totally different way than we do. Numbers don't matter to God. We know that He is the shepherd that leaves his 99 to go after the one, count it out, one, sheep. So maybe He is looking at the hearts that are changed rather than the measurable results we are used to looking at.

Bottom line is this: succeed or fail, obedience to God is always a sign of spiritual strength. Whatever else you may feel or think about something, know that if you were obedient, you did the right thing.

Deuteronomy 11:1, 2 Corinthians 10:5, John 15:14

Dear God, please help me today to not feel like a failure. Give me Your eyes to see what is true about my success and failure, and help me to not judge myself with human measurements. Lord, I pray that

You would give me an understanding of Your plan for my obedience, and patience with myself as I discover Your grace. Thank you for teaching me through obedience, and for always walking with me. I love you so, Jesus! For all these things I pray in Your mighty name Jesus. Amen.

...maybe, just maybe, the obedience was the victory...

Shut Your Mouth

What do you say when you don't know what to say? All those times people are pouring their hearts out and you are mentally searching your catalog of words, what comes out?

Can we all agree that when we are the one doing the heart revealing, the last thing we need/want is a lecture, a sermon, or a miniseries about the time someone else went through it!

What we need is for our audience to have a listening ear, a big hug, and chocolate. Just kidding about the chocolate. Kind of. But seriously, sometimes, it's okay to not have words. I am becoming more and more okay with silence, and its raw power.

When we watch a political debate, which candidate is the loser? The one that talks too much. When we sit through a sermon that drags on and on, who are we feeling grouchy at? The minister who didn't keep his message simple and succinct. When we are sitting in an office meeting and someone keeps talking, disregarding everyone else that is trying to get out and get home to family, who are all the dagger glares on? You guessed it, the motor mouth.

Today, practice keeping quiet when you can. Watch the power that you have in your words Friend!

Proverbs 17:27-28, Ecclesiastes 3:7, James 1:19

J.O.Y. Life Challenge:

Compliment a stranger today. Watch as they brighten with your kind words. Make an effort to take this challenge into tomorrow as well, and every day until it is common practice.

$\mathcal{L}$ies, Rejection and Dimples

Growing up, I heard people say that dimples were where angels had kissed cheeks before babes were sent to earth.

This was a problem for me, because I have three sisters and they all have two perfect dimples on their cheeks. But I only have one. One dimple. One angel kiss?

Even now, I still have moments when I see their perfect dimpled cheeks and a feeling of loss surges in my gut. I was jealous when I was younger, but that wore off a long time ago. Now, just the thought of only getting ONE kiss haunts me! Even as I type this, I know how silly it sounds.

The reason I am sharing this embarrassing truth is because I can't possibly be the only person feeling some sort of internal grumbling over a fable! We've got to get a grasp on reality people. There are enough real life struggles to face head first that need our attention; let's leave these ridiculous wishes for what could've been, should've been, might be. Today is full of real opportunities to overcome real obstacles. I am going to grin and bear it, with my lonely dimple on display. Because overcoming the struggles I face with Jesus, brings me true joy!

What lies are haunting you to this day, making you feel less than, small or lacking value?

John 17:17, Psalm 43:3, Ephesians 4:25

Oh Jesus, sweet King. These lies, these stories have been haunting me for my entire life. Can You help me face them and call them on their bluff, this very day? Free me Jesus, from the pain and hurt that I am carrying through this weighty shackle. Give me a truth, a real promise that You have honored through the ages to cling to as I move away from these strongholds, and help me, as I know that the struggle I face will not be easily ended. Thank you, loving Jesus. I love you! For all these things I pray in Your mighty name Jesus.

Let's leave these ridiculous wishes for what could've been, should've been, might be.

Talk to Him

My husband flew to Africa a few years ago for a mission trip. Due to the distance, cost of international calls, lack of internet and time difference I only spoke to him three or four times in a 10 day stretch. Each night as I tried to fall asleep, I longed to hear his voice and to tell him about my day and hear about his.

It was like Christmas when he got home and I could finally hear him again. Our relationships have so much more vitality when we communicate with each other regularly. The same goes for our relationship with God! We have to pray continually in order to have a meaningful relationship with our Heavenly Father. Can you begin a dialogue with Him today that you carry through all your busy-ness?

1 Thessalonians 5:17, Psalm 145:18

Dear God today is full of planned activities, and I am sure there will be more than enough activity to distract me from You. Can You help me to remember to focus on You and share my needs with You today? Father, I love that You want to hear me, and that You are always close at hand. Guide me today Lord, I ask in Jesus' name. Amen.

Ruth's Radical Life

When I was 15, I met this shaggy haired, rebellious, mouthy young man. He wasn't a particularly good person, and we didn't like each other. Here I was this goody-two-shoes kind of gal, with a strict plan for my future and my life. This plan certainly didn't include any blue haired, heavy metal band wannabes. I never would have believed then that he would become the second half of me; my husband, the father to my children, the hero when I am weak, my companion amid the chaos.

My friends, some of life's greatest surprises come from a place we aren't looking. Maybe today you'll find yourself seeking fulfillment or joy from something, when in all reality, the things you might not like or appreciate (those trials!!) are a real source of health and life for you.

My favorite biblical story is that of Ruth, and her mother in love Naomi. Ruth had it *rough*. With a capital "R." Yet she never doubted that God would show up in her trials, evident by her lack of complaining and her incredible bravery and persistence.

If you have time today, read the book of Ruth (its only four quick chapters).

God, I see some tough places in my life. I realize that the obnoxious aspects of them might offer me the opportunity to grow stronger and closer to You. Help me today, Father. I need Your help to face these moments, people, situations, because without You they are impossible. I love you Father, and I trust You to give me what I can handle today and every day. Amen.

Some of life's greatest surprises come from a place we aren't looking.

Strength in Numbers

Life can come at us leaving us feeling so emotionally exhausted that we cannot always find our way back alone. We need God. We need family, friends and the gift of community. All of the greatest acts of love and accomplishment are completed by teams, never an individual.

In the book of Genesis we read that God did not believe that man needed to be alone, so He created a partner. Y'all, Adam was chilling in the Garden of Eden with God, but it wasn't enough. And God Himself saw that, thus giving us humanity, rather than one lonely man.

Perhaps you are going through something so painful and embarrassing that you do not feel like you should or could burden someone else with it. Think again. You can't do it alone. You will fail. Yeah, you might make decisions that help you survive, but you will fall apart a little more each day that goes by, whereas if you had a partner, a friend, a fellow, you might just be able to face off against the giants that are tearing you down without breaking much of a sweat.

And one last thing, maybe your life is peachy. Maybe you feel free and clear after reading that last paragraph. But you're wrong. Someone you love, or at least know, needs you. They crave your prayers, time, and company. Don't let them down because you are comfortable. Follow the example of Jesus, who came and walked among men, and love on the others in your life.

Philippians 2:3, Ecclesiastes 4:9-12

J.O.Y. Life Challenge:

Pick one person to pray for specifically, and ask them to do the same for you. Ask your prayer partner how you can help them, surprise them with little moments of joy in the form of a simple gift, a quiet hug, a trusted shoulder to cry one, a warm cup of tea. Don't give up; be faithful to that person as long as God has convicted you to.

You can't do it alone.

20/20 Vision

From my youngest childhood, I remember thinking glasses were a symbol of attractiveness. I wanted glasses, and badly. Every year, I'd look at the little letters on the chart, and try as I might, I couldn't make them blurry. I read each letter, with no problems. Even today, I am glasses free. Only now can I see what my younger self was oblivious to: 20/20 vision is a gift and one I should be grateful for. We know that as we look back at our lives, there are so many times we wanted unhealthy things for ourselves. The old cliché goes, "Hindsight is 20/20," right?

I think of the biblical story of Jonah, whenever I consider this blindness of mine to the gift of my good vision. This guy was such a fool. And he paid dearly. God sent him a tough mission, I will give him that. But he ran scared, until his only option was to die or submit to God's plan for his life. Figuratively, I think we are all there, at some point.

Is there anything you are looking for that may be holding you back? A vision that is founded on some unhealthy desire, perhaps? God knows us best; never be afraid to seek Him if you find yourself yearning for glasses and passing all those vision tests!

If you have the time, read the book of Jonah today. If not, read Jonah's prayer, found in Jonah 2:1-9.

God, can You help me today to see clearly the vision You have for my life? I have this plan that I have pursued, but I want to live according to Your plan. Help me to have Your vision today and every day and to pursue it with all the vigor and excitement that I have pursued my own missions. Please forgive me, Lord, for not honoring You with my obedience and offering my plans to You. I love you Lord. Amen.

Find Him in His Word

Vision is often blurred by the here and now. We see things so often as they are, not as they are going to be with lots of prayer and hard work. As a wife, I want there to be a vision for my marriage that is more than meal preparation and obligatory kisses on the cheek when my husband gets home. As a mother, I want to have sight into the plans God has for my children, beyond the day to day monotony of diaper changing and discipline. As a child of God, I want to see that I am not just some Sunday morning tally on a chart, but rather a living, breathing tool used to worship with my existence. I want clear sight, and nowhere do I get so much inspiration as I do when I open my Bible.

Frightening statistics are out there that show the number of Bible reading people is shrinking so fast it's going to be a tiny minority before too long if we don't fall back in love with God's word. Can you find vision today in His spoken word?

Proverbs 3:5-6, Joshua 1:8

J.O.Y. Life Challenge:

Try to read for just five minutes a day until you find yourself working up to 10, and then add as you can. This is not something that we can ignore without expecting true consequences.

Freedom from Passing Judgement

We have all heard the age old, "Judge not lest ye be judged," speech, am I right? But is there anyone else out there that finds this incredibly difficult?

I try not to focus too much on what Christians do wrong namely because I believe that if people are drawing close to God, He takes care of the weaknesses in their character and attitudes through His own means. Essentially, it's His holy business to take up with His people, and so long as I am letting Him work in me, there is no need for me to dwell on what He does in and through others excepting to encourage and lift up my fellow brethren in Christ.

But friends, there are so many people out there that are not following Christ. It can be downright impossible not to cast a wary look at the behavior of those different from us. My mother always told me not to judge a non-Christian by Christian standards. And I would urge you to take my mama's advice today. Not because I think you are going out there and passing judgment on everyone you see, but because it is freedom not to walk around with a plank in one's eye if you can catch my drift.

Matthew 7:3, 1 Corinthians 5:12

Father God, You know that I am not perfect. So do I. It's difficult to admit, especially when other people are driving me crazy. But Jesus, You went through this and I know You must have felt the urge to need to be right. To win. Lord, I know that You have already won the war, and today, I want to just dwell in that. Help me to release my futile judgements of others. Give me a renewed spirit, that I might share my freedom with others. I love you Lord, and I thank you for leading me with grace when I am not deserving of it. I pray for all of these things to come to pass, in the name of Jesus, Amen.

What's and Who's

When I look in the mirror I almost always see a "what," as opposed to a precious "whom." Graying hair, blemished skin, and a body that is less and less firm and toned each day etc. But God, when looking at us, sees a person. A child He created joyfully. Just like those precious first moments when my sons discovered themselves in the mirror and I had tears of joy well up due to my love for them, so does God want us to see ourselves not as a collection of whats, but as a precious, remarkable WHO! You are not a what. God has a vision for you, precious one!

Books, speaking tours, sermons, and countless messages have been put out there that can help a person discover their destiny in Christ, what they are supposed to do with their life, and how to meet maximum potential. But Friend, it's not that complicated.

He has been trying to tell you your whole life, through the series of events He orchestrated and the natural gifts He gave you. Look to Him for answers, and know right this second, that if you had any doubt this morning when you woke up, you were created in love by God for a specific plan.

Psalm 139:14, Romans 12:6-8

God, thank you for creating me. Thank you for every moment I have lived so far; the painful as well as the near perfect. God, I know that You have brought me together and through these events with such a plan that I can not even fathom and I pray fervently that You would open my eyes in proportion to my maturity. Let me see what I can handle of my destiny, and help me to grow each day that I am more fully aware of You in me all the days of my life. I love you Lord Jesus! Amen.

*L*iving Water

I have a dog and a cat. Neither of them chooses to drink out of a water bowl. The cat will *only* drink out of the faucet or, on occasion, out of a human drinking glass(but only if there is ice water within). The dog drinks out of the toilet, puddles, sand pails, and all sorts of other suspect vessels, but never the water bowl we have beside his food bowl. I was walking the dog and bemoaning this one night. Right after his walk, I came in and the cat meowed until I turned on her precious faucet. These two drive me crazy!

Here I am putting out clean, healthy, appropriate water for them every day and they never want to drink it. God is going to put out clean, life giving sustenance for you every day. There will be plenty of other vessels to drink out of to get your stamina, joy, will power, etc. But honestly, upon closer inspection, these other sources are probably no better for you than toilet water or standing water from an old puddle. Look for His living water each day, Friend!

John 4:14

God, You are so good to be there every day, offering me the chance to live a healthy, pure life by Your side. Thank you for the endless opportunities for vitality. Please help me to see Your sustenance today, in the many different places You offer it. I want to choose Your living water today, and every day. I love you Lord!

Victory through Christ

People who break out of the mold expected for their life are some of the most heroic individuals in our world; the young man who statistics say should be imprisoned by his 21st birthday but instead sticks to the straight and narrow and earns a degree instead; the woman who is destined to live off of men and never see her full potential realized in a career or education, who goes and swears them off until she gets her life situated with a future for hope; the family of a certain religion that finds Christ and, despite all dangers and odds, converts to follow Him all their days. These are remarkable people, real life unsung heroes. There are people in your own life who have broken cycles, and maybe you are one yourself! Relish the victory that humanity has been given through Christ!

Who is a hero to you? Why are they so important? Can you honor that person and their efforts today?

Proverbs 19:1, Isaiah 33:15-16

J.O.Y. Life Challenge:

My kids and I spend one day a month making a meal for our local heroes. We choose 12 groups of people or individuals who have inspired, protected, preserved and loved us and make them food. We also write them a thank you card, and these two small acts are such a joy for us. They also bring Jesus to the others in our life. Give it a try one day!

Relish the victory that humanity has been given through Christ!

*P*ity Party Patrol

My human propensity to fall back into old ways can shock me sometimes. I am not a whiner by nature. Growing up, I heard on the regular, "Suck it up, Buttercup!" Complaining was, and is, my mother's pet peeve.

People who don't complain do one thing very well. That one thing is called throwing a pity party. Party music, closely resembling fussy sighs, is repeated; decorations appear in the form of fake smiles and hollow, distant looks, and the theme of the party is always, "Poor, poor me."

Some of us are good at managing the guest list for our pity parties, letting only one or maybe two others form the very elite "who's who." Others let the whole world in on the struggle, venting through social media or large audiences. But is this the kind of party that I need to be throwing?

When I let my own life struggles keep me down, I am practicing a form of pride. I am saying that my own inability to move on is more important than letting God heal me, change me, grow me. There is no humility in my pity parties, just pride. God doesn't mind our worries, fears, frustrations and angst. On the contrary, He welcomes them. But we have to GIVE them to Him, we can't hold on. We have to let go. We have to break that pattern.

Ephesians 4:2, Isaiah 23:9, James 4:6

J.O.Y. Life Challenge:

I can't say it enough: write it down. Angry at someone or something? Heartbroken? Aghast? Write it in a journal. Vent there, to the opinion-less paper that can not judge you, will not criticize you, and will be your friend the next day. Once it's written down, think about freeing yourself from the any lingering thoughts by offering both the thoughts you penned and the ones left over to the Lord in prayer.

When I let my own life struggles keep me down, I am practicing a form of pride.

The Humility of Jesus

Maybe it is the thought of Mary and Joseph cradling little Jesus in their arms, but I can't seem to shake the humbling responsibility of parenthood. Parenting is humbling because children could care less about qualifications. They simply want to know who is going to feed them, play with them, and love them. They add insult to injury by coming up with new and fantastic ways to shock and astound us into early old age and graying hair. Worst of all though, is that they have no idea how our spirits are so tied to their little lives. It hurts to an unimaginable level when they are hurting and there is nothing we can do for them except pray. It is almost crippling to see them struggle through their trials and patiently wait on them to figure out how to *be* in a world that doesn't always accept.

There has never been a time in my life when I was as dependent on God as when I became a mother. I cannot do much of anything for these children on my own. Nothing lasting or legacy building anyway. I need God, and that is humbling because the days I go out without giving Him that nod of, "Please, lead me," all the horrors take over.

So I think about God as our heavenly father. And I think about patterns. And I realize that God, my God, is so awe-inspiring because He too is a humble father. He doesn't assert His will on my life, but waits patiently for me to come to Him, when I am aware of my need for Him. Like me as a mother, He covets those slobbery kisses and octopus body hugs. He craves that moment when I put down my play things and climb into His lap for wise counsel. He is humble that we too might learn to be.

Ephesians 3:14-15, Proverbs 11:2

God, I have people who depend on me. They need me to be strong, loving, kind, honest, true and loyal. They need me to be something that I can't be without You leading me. Please, guide me, that I might be humble and full of light through this challenging day. Help me to choose to be the best I can be for those that You have given me to shepherd, and show me how to be Your hands and feet today. I love you Lord. For all these things I pray in Your mighty name Jesus. Amen.

He is humble that we too might learn to be.

Intentionally Quiet

There are days when I choose to be intentionally quiet. This isn't like a "library voice" quiet. This is a concentrated effort to soak in my surroundings at the expense of my racing thoughts and mouth. I don't know about you, but when days come up that are particularly riddled with newness, whether good or bad, my tendency, is to jump all in and get stuff done. My senses are tuned to the experience, and I don't think about much else but conquering the task at hand. This is good, and bad. It's good because stuff gets done, but it is bad because I am often missing the blessings that came about or will come about due to the moment.

That's where the quiet comes in. Listening to the Lord through newness, whether it's positive or negative change, helps us hear what is most important. One quiet day, I recall the ample blessings that came from my silence. On that day, my husband went through surgery and it couldn't have been a better operation. The staff at the hospital was fantastic. I got chocolate. God spoke to me through each little interaction, "I have this, just hold close to my hand." And that's just what I wish I did all the time. I wish I could break all my normal patterns and simply hold His hand.

1 Samuel 12:16, Psalm 62: 5-6, Exodus 14:14

J.O.Y. Life Challenge:

Practice quiet moments throughout your day. When you go to log onto email/social media/news/television, etc. choose instead to contemplate your life. Where is God working in your days? What changes are happening that you can practice quiet in?

Daily Redemption

I've heard a lot about pattern sin in my life, and I want to talk about that for a moment. There is a pattern to our flawed humanity, both individually and corporately as the body of Christ. We keep messing up in the same ways. While one person may be prone to lying and exaggerating, another may be prone to pride and stubbornness against God (spiritual rebellion). We act like the Syrian refugee crisis is one of the worst horrors in history, but there was a very similar pattern to the treatment of Jewish people when they fled persecution during World War II. The sin pattern of war and murder, theft and greed continues to be seen throughout history.

So if we keep messing up, over and over, in a pattern that is probably more predictable than we realize, where is God? Where does His son, Jesus, stand in the midst of our pattern sin? Take joy my Friend, because though it may be difficult to see how and where at times, God has a redemption pattern that is even more powerful and impressive than our continual sin.

Every time His people come to Him on their hands and knees with a spirit of repentance, He forgives. Every. Time. Is there a pattern sin in your life today, keeping you from moving forward with Christ? Does it seem innocent enough, or too small to bother quitting? Or does it seem so huge that you doubt you can give it up because it is such a part of you that you don't know how to live without it?

God sees. He feels the pain, the pressure, and He cares whether it seems large or small, because sin keeps Him away. And He wants to be so close to you.

Ephesians 1:7, Titus 2:14

God, there are no words to express how great You are. And that can seem overpowering at times, especially when I feel so small and especially when I am wrong. Can You help me today Lord? I need You to forgive me for my sins (take time to name those specific things here). Can You forgive me, wiping my spirit clean with the perfect blood of Jesus, that I might be free of this burden? Thank you Jesus.

Please, help now as I try to break this pattern of sin in my life. I need You to help me, Jesus! Replace my desires and impulses for what is wrong, in order that I do what is right. I want You close to me, Father, forever! I love you, Lord. For all these things I pray in Your mighty name Jesus. Amen.

His Sacrifice, Our Inspiration

As an explorer of God's Word, I have discovered a long running pattern of pain and suffering that the men and women of God must face. The most physically and emotionally challenging experience of my life has been childbirth. Under the heavy influence of pain and struggle, one thought recurred in my mental loop as I labored to bring my boys into this world.

Jesus died on the cross for me.

He selflessly embraced His agony, which carried the weight of every human to ever come after Him and their sins. This truth gave me an anchor for my suffering in labor and delivery, and it does each and every moment that I encounter the enemy and his attacks on my life.

Jesus was still holding onto the joy He had in store when He completed His work on the cross. He must have envisioned embracing all the broken people who would fall into His arms in heaven one day. I can just see His face muscles taut with extreme exhaustion, pain and sadness transforming each moment He neared His death, those features relaxing more and more, until He crested that darkness and completed His mission.

As God molds us and shapes us, His vision for our life will take us through storms, there is no question of it, my Friend. But we must hold onto the hope that comes after the storm has ended. We are working through our hurdles to a higher and more lasting blessing than we know. Don't give up, Friend!

1 Corinthians 9:24, 2 Timothy 4:7

Dear God, I am being rammed on so many fronts. My energy is failing, my desire to complete my mission is lost, and I am holding on by a thread in these areas (tell God about your dark places). Lord, please help me to stay strong, and focus on the prize of completing my mission one day and joining You in heaven. God, You are hope, and joy, and peace and light. Please fill me with Your son's strength today. In Jesus' name I pray for these things. Amen.

Jesus died on the cross for me.

No Such Thing as a Coincidence

Coincidences don't exist. Sure, you and your neighbor might wear the same size shoe and type of socks, but if you happen upon this little detail don't you think that's an opportunity to follow a conversation and build a relationship? Any and all outlandish circumstances seem to me to be an opportunity to learn and grow relationships.

Recently, I went to visit a friend who had just given birth, but somehow I ended up at the wrong hospital! Chastising myself under my breath in the elevator, I almost didn't notice a couple sitting off to the side of the lobby, trying to keep warm. It was a chilly April day with a fierce spring breeze blowing through my sweater and layered shirts.

The couple approached me as I neared them; they were both dressed in shabby attire, dirty and shared a ripe fragrance. When they got close to me, they asked for some money to purchase food. As a rule, I don't hand out money, but I did offer to get them dinner.

God placed some hungry, likely homeless people, right in front of me. Was it coincidental that I was at the wrong hospital while they were looking for dinner? Nope. It was a character building moment for me. Some hungry people got fed, and all I lost out on was an hour of my time. What was gained was another opportunity to seek relationship with God as I paused to serve.

What coincidences has God placed in your life recently that, once inspected, might be an opportunity to see God at work?

Ephesians 1:11, Romans 8:28

God, I want to take time to thank you for all the intricate details You have placed in my life. Help me to see Your handiwork more and more each day as these little miracles are occurring. Father, I want to be able to celebrate the miraculous; help me to slow down so that I might see the beautiful moments before me and know they are gifts that You have given to me. Your gifts are wonderful, and so is Your plan, Holy God! Thank you for loving me and planning an amazing path for my life. In Jesus name I pray for these things. Amen.

$\mathcal{J}$t Matters

One day, I was feeling blah; a real sense of apathy had come into my spirit and taken over. In a particularly whiny voice, I shared with my husband,

"I feel like all I ever do is cook for people and clean the mess and then go through the whole thing all over again."

Attempting to celebrate rest in my life, I sat down later with a magazine. The only article I had time to read gave me goosebumps. A woman had given birth to a preterm baby, and people fed her family. Every night, for three months, someone would arrive with a hot meal so that this mother could check that off of her list giving her a few extra minutes a day to spend with her tiny child at the hospital where she was in care. Of all the support she had gotten, the meals were what meant the most, the author of the article explained.

In that moment I felt in my heart God's message to me: "It matters, every bite you give to others matters." My Friend, take joy, because your time devoted in service to others is seen by God, and it really does matter!

Matthew 23:11, 1 Peter 4:10

Dear, sweet Jesus, who came from Your place in heaven to serve us here on earth, I invite You to teach me today. Let me learn from Your example of how to serve others in love and kindness. Lord, You know that all this service can make me feel like I am running around aimlessly. Help me to see the joys in servanthood today Father! Thank you for every opportunity to serve. I love you and ask that You would cover these needs with Your precious name, Jesus. Amen.

God Keeps His Promises

We can't choose for our kids to follow Jesus. Or our spouses. Or our friends. But we can believe and trust His word to be true. There is a promise in the Bible that explicitly states that if we believe and trust in our Lord Jesus, not only will we be saved, but so will our households.

The specifics are a little foggy here. And I think it's important to mention that it's foolish to think that just because our grandmothers had Jesus as their Lord and Savior, we are somehow saved. Our salvation is ours alone, not old Granny's. There must have been someone that had a light that shone brightly into your life at some point. Our spiritual attraction to the Light of the World, through whoever shines it brightly, is a huge part of God's plan.

We need to shine our light to our community in the same way. How can you shine so brightly that your witness stands as evidence of God to those around you that do not yet believe? While I trust that God holds His promises true every time, I also believe that I must be active in my faith if I want to see this scripture come to pass. Be active today, my loves! Let your belief in God's promises fuel you to overflow all throughout this day. Be kind. Speak uplifting words. Smile. Forgive. Watch God take those simple things and turn over amazing acts of change.

Acts 16:31, John 14:12-14, John 3:16

J.O.Y. Life Challenge:

Reach out to Granny, or whoever it was that first showed you the love of Jesus. Thank them for the specific things that they did in your life to help you see the joy available in having Jesus as your savior. Then go and be like Granny to whoever God has placed in your life!

Wired to Fight

Lately the disaster that pornography has created in our global society has infiltrated my life. I have had to tackle the sad effects of this evil one too many times in working with youth and young adults. The aftermath is rocky at best and devastating at worst. The struggle with addiction to pornography has repeatedly popped up in the lives of men and women all around me. Pastors, spiritual leaders, the young and old alike have been lured in by the tremendous pressures of this sneaky horror, and it breaks my heart. Every time.

In life, there are things we are specifically wired to fight. Perhaps the horrors of the effects of pornography isn't something you take issue with, but what gets under your skin? What makes you queasy with anger and sadness? What are you doing to change that issue? Be brave today Friend; you have the power to change the world! Do not give up today, but stay the course and begin a journey of changing lives, one person at a time, in whatever area you know in your heart you are called to.

Ephesians 6:12, Romans 8

J.O.Y. Life Challenge:

There are so many great books and resources out there on creating a battle plan against the evils that we see being acted out all around us. We need a battle plan, too. What is the cause that God has given you to take up? Take time today to acknowledge it, embrace it, and begin a journey creating a battle plan with God to conquer it. You can change the world, Friend. Never doubt that!

Heavenly Focus

Do you think of heaven often? Honestly, I don't. And that's a problem. When my days are so long and so filled with hard work, there is nothing more inspiring and stimulating than the thought of *a perfect eternity*.

No more cancer. No more disease, period. No more slavery. No more child abuse. No more elderly neglect. No more homelessness. No more starvation. No more war. No more theft. No more fighting. No more exhaustion. No more cruelty. No more hurtful words. No more anger. No more sadness. No more…Can you imagine?

All of that will be replaced with perfection. The most perfect moments in my life, all of them, have still had a measure of difficulty. My wedding day was riddled with little mishaps. Holding my kids for the first time in my arms? It was amazing and wonderful each time, but there were still some major difficulties overshadowing each of those events. Seeing major projects completed? Even then, when I have been confident of my performance, there is always the creeping thought of, "What's next?"

But Heaven, oh it will be so different! It will be *perfect*. My son took a picture of the sky on my phone recently. It was all blue, forever, except in the corner of the photo. There was a patch of blinding white light coming in and somehow this little image captured my heart for heaven again. It reminded me that there is so much goodness waiting to take over, just as that light was piercing the blue. I am so glad to have been reminded that this life isn't the only thing we were made for. May the inspiration of heaven take you through this day and many hard moments, Friend!

Revelation 21:4, Romans 10:9-13

J.O.Y. Life Challenge:

There is confidence of heaven for those that have asked Jesus to be their Lord and savior, and have followed the steps laid out in Romans 10:9-13. Have you accepted Jesus as your Savior? Do you need to? If so, please pray the following with all your heart:

"Lord God, I know that I have broken Your laws and that my own mistakes and sins have kept me away from You. Today I am so very sorry for each of those moments. Here and now I want to change my life, and turn from those old ways of doing wrong. Forgive me, as Your Holy Word says that You will, and protect me on all sides. Help me, Lord, to avoid sin. I believe that Your son, Jesus Christ, died for my sins, was resurrected from the dead, is alive, and hears my prayer. I ask that You, Jesus, would become my Lord and savior today, to live and reign in my heart for the rest of my life. Lord, please send the Holy Spirit to guide me and keep me close to You. In Jesus' name I pray, Amen."

*This life isn't the only
thing we were made for.*

Uniquely and Wonderfully Made

God made us each uniquely. There has never been, nor will there ever be, another you. That is because you were specially created for a purpose. There are days that the best thing the enemy can do is make you doubt yourself. If you doubt yourself, you will be pretty busy fretting. And if you are busy fretting, you are not using your energy to trust in God and you certainly aren't actively pursuing the mission He has for your life.

Don't be fooled today Friend. Ignore the lies. You are good enough. Strong enough. Able enough. Whatever it is that you lack, you can trust God to have in abundance. You were created for a purpose. No lies of the enemy will ever change that. Listen for God's commands on your life, and use your individuality to make your life the work of art He intended!

Psalm 119:73, Galatians 6:4

Dear God, please help me to hear Your voice louder than the voice of the evil one today. Help me to ignore the lies, the hurts, the failures, the lacking places. Let me see me the way that You see me! I want so badly to walk with You, trusting Your plan for my life. I love you Lord, and I thank you that You had a special mission in store for me before I even came to this earth. You are wondrous, and I praise You today! In the mighty name of Jesus I pray, Amen.

There has never been, nor will there ever be, another you.

"I Did It"

You know that feeling you get when your to-do list is a mile long but all the energy you can scrape up is enough to write the list? And then you are mad at yourself for not getting anything done? Life demands that we are so busy. We must temper our activity with life giving rest. There was a commandment to rest on the Sabbath because God knew we needed to be told to do it or we would never be still long enough to recuperate from our output of energy.

If you feel like you are running around with not a moment's peace in sight, maybe now is a good time to pause. Take a deep breath. Consider God's plan for your day, rather than your own. That lack of energy may be exhaustion begging you to take ear to its pleas for time off. Today, Let God carry your burdens. Let Him shoulder the weight of your busy-ness. Rest, knowing that no matter what you do or don't do, God is with you!

Psalm 127:2, Exodus 33:14, Matthew 11:28-30

J.O.Y. Life Challenge:

Make an "I Did It" list. What did you accomplish today? Write it down! It's usually more than you think!

Rest, knowing that no matter what you do or don't do, God is with you!

Finding Joy in Your Calling

My oldest son started his second season of little league baseball recently. He has a lot of potential, but truthfully, he spends just as much time charming the crowds and goofing off as he does playing baseball. I had four different people come up to me in the span of the game to say, "You're not going to believe what Kiernan just said..."

As we were talking about his behavior like it was a problem last night, it suddenly hit my husband and me that maybe Kiernan won't ever be an MLB MVP. But if he is using the gifts God gave Him to brighten the world, who am I to sit around and worry about what my son ISN'T doing?

Instead of worrying about what He didn't come to earth to fix, Jesus was incredibly intentional. His focus was solely on what God sent Him to do. Nowhere in scripture does it say, "Then Jesus sat around and worried if His disciples had attention deficit disorder and if He should have them checked by the local doctor."

Rather, Jesus encouraged His disciples to be the men that God designed them to be. So today, if you are worrying about what you aren't getting done in your life, let yourself off the hook (and the people around you too!). Instead, try to focus on what you were made to do and get that thing done. Encourage it in others as well. May you have *joy* today!

John 14:6, John 5:30

Dear Father, I need You today. I need You to remind me that I am here because You are so gracious and full of love for Your people that You would use me for Your plan, when You have the entire universe at Your disposal. Give me the grace to share this revelation with those around me today. I want to encourage others to be their best, just as You have encouraged me to be my best. I love you Lord, and I thank you for this today. I love you Jesus! It's in Your precious name that I pray. Amen.

Jesus was incredibly intentional.

Investments and Dividends

After I gave birth to my third son, I entered into that sleep deprived, blurry minded existence that I have come to understand as normal the first few weeks and months after a baby is welcomed into a family.

When the adjustment period wound down, I replaced my necessary naps and coffee breaks with more and more quiet time. While before I was desperate for physical replenishment, the cycle changed and I sought more and more spiritual refreshment through reading books about God and spiritual training, my Bible, coloring(yes, I picked up that fad), listening to more music, and writing.

Most of all, in this process, I am saw yet again, that what we invest into something, we get in return. There were many changes happening in my life at that time, but because I prioritized building peace into my daily schedule, I slowly discovered my still heart amidst the busyness and newness I faced each day. All this is to say, that whatever you invest in, is going to pay you back, usually with some sort of dividends.

So what are you investing in? Jesus invested His entire life into doing what God sent Him to Earth to do. That's what I want to accomplish. Nothing more, and nothing less, because that is enough.

Matthew 6:19-21, 2 Corinthians 9:6

Lord God, I want to take a look at my investments today. Can You help me in this quiet time appraise my spiritual growth and where I have spent my most valuable resources of time, energy, spirit, and love? (Pause and listen for God's wisdom.)

Help me today Father, to be a savvy business person with the matters of my spirit. Give me the insight to hear the people around me, and to serve them with my hands and feet. Give me Your heart Jesus, that I might serve humbly and with great fortitude. Thank you for this time, Father. I love you! For all these things, I pray in Jesus name. Amen.

The Healing Power of Forgiveness

While Jesus was dying on the cross, He called out to God, "Father, forgive them. They know not what they do."

I always find this part of the crucifixion story remarkable. There He was, God in man, being humiliated and tortured, asking for forgiveness for His torturers. One of my heroines is Corrie Ten Boom, a woman who survived the horrible treatment of Nazis in the worst prison camp in WWII history. After she was freed, she began a ministry to forgive and encourage former Nazis. At times, she even crossed paths with her former captors.

Corrie watched her father and sister die in camp. But when she met with these former torturers, she managed to forgive and even asked God to free them of their guilt. If a little old lady who went through that kind of hell on earth, and could honor and imitate Jesus Christ, surely we can extend love for others in abundance today!

Who has God placed in your life as a particular thorn in your side? How can you look at them with God's eyes? In what way can you extend grace, forgiveness, love and kindness today Friend?

John 13:34, Philippians 2:3-4, Micah 6:8

Father God, I think of the "others" in my life and I cringe at times! Some of these people have hurt me deeply, and some are just such a heavy load to carry through my life. Today, can You bring clarity to me, and help me to see Your plan in placing these people in my life? I need to be refreshed with Your love in order to love others this very moment, God. I thank you for sending Jesus to die for me, that I would be able to see and feel His outpouring of pure love each day. I love you, Jesus! For all this I pray in His Holy Name. Amen.

ℒetting Go and Letting God

Lately my heart has been breaking. I have seen so many posts on social media, overheard many conversations and witnessed many accounts of believers attempting to "lovingly" explain what is right and wrong to others.

Sin should bother us, as believers in Jesus, primarily because it signifies a separation from Him. Our goal is never to change others, but to love them as Jesus with the expectation that His influence in their lives will be the catalyst for redemption. Jesus was perfect; therefore I contend to all believers to let Him sort out sin within the hearts that you are filling up with love and care. He is far more capable in His perfection of performing this task than we will ever be.

While we are to lead by example and to honor God by living lives devoid of sin, as best we can, there is no health or life that comes from lecturing, chastising, proselytizing, or preaching if the audience doesn't first feel loved and wanted.

Ephesians 4:2, Matthew 7:1-5

J.O.Y. Life Challenge:

Today, a lot of people are turned off to Christianity because of the judgmental eyes they sense watching them. Can you take a stand for loving others by creating a moment of kindness for someone in your life today? How can you continue to pursue them with the love of Jesus? Don't pick a stranger, be specific. Who can you lovingly serve and show Jesus' passion towards?

Sin should bother us, as believers in Jesus, primarily because it signifies a separation from Him.

But God...

People can be pathetic, in the highest sense of the word. They always have been, and always will be...**But God.**

Murderers, sexual predators, violent criminals, thieves and slanderers walk among us, and it can seem that there is no justice...**But God.**

People spout off disgusting untruths and cruelties until it seems as if there is no decency left in the world...**But God.**

But God sent Jesus- to fix all this mucky-muck. It may not seem like He did much when we look out into the world today, but we must take heart, Friend. Jesus' life should bring us peace and joy, even amidst the suffering, with the knowledge that though there is still great darkness, His light will overcome all the evil, forever.

John 16:33, 1 John 5:4, Romans 8:31

Dear Father, hold me in Your arms today. Help me to feel Your protection and safety. I know that You have overcome this world, and I thank you from the depths of my soul for Your strength and wonderful love. I feel fear at times, anxiety at others and unrest- often. I need You to replace these with confidence in my victory as Your child. I love you Lord, and I thank you for touching me today with Your fierce victory. In Jesus name I pray, Amen.

$\mathcal{P}$leasing the Heavenly Father

I am the oldest of four girls, and growing up in a large family was a lot of fun. There are some struggles that can come with being the oldest child; the greatest of these for me was the pressure I felt to always set a good example. As a child, I wanted to please my parents and help the family dynamic run as smooth as possible. This desire to set a good example left my parents' home with me, and has continued into my adult life, where it took some hard knocks to realize that I am never going to please everyone, and I need to hone my need to please my Heavenly Father.

Jesus was a first born of a big brood, too. I imagine that He had many of the same experiences I did. He must have laughed through loud dinners, had plenty of built in playmates, and I know He endured the pressure to perform as an oldest child. But His goal was always to please His Heavenly Father.

Even as a small child, when He stayed behind on a "vacation" and spoke to rabbis when He should have been setting a good example for His younger siblings, He was pursuing God. His parents chastised Him, but in His heart He knew that He had done what was right. No matter who you feel pressure to perform for today, and every day, remember that God is the ultimate judge. We don't have to live by our parents' (or friends' or loved ones') standards. If they don't align with God's this is doubly true! We just have to wake up each day as eager children, excited to please the Father who loves us unconditionally.

Hebrews 11:6, 1 Thessalonians 2:4

Dear God, seeking the approval of other people can be such a toxic, addictive drug that I can get caught up before I realize how far I have gone down a dangerous path. Can You help me today to change my heart? I need my heart to want Your approval more than it wants to please the other people around me. I know this will mean changes in my life; changes that might even hurt as I grow. Forgive me Father, for choosing to pursue fleeting approval and for forgetting You as my first love. Today, I want to change in order to draw near to You. I love you Lord, and I thank you for always seeing in me something worthy of Your approval. In Jesus' name I pray, Amen.

Get Out of the Office

I've been blessed to work in ministry. Hands down the best part of working in ministry is watching what God does in the lives of people who choose to follow Him. However, as I am not as active a professional as I'd like to be these days, I've come to terms with the fact that God still uses me, and He is still doing amazing things that I can be a part of, outside of an office building or a church.

Jesus' disciples experienced something similar. Here were these fishermen, called to leave their "office" to enter a new field of work, and there, they would continue to use the skills they had acquired throughout their life, just for a whole new pursuit.

Many of us hold degrees in a given field, or have a skill set we worked hard to develop. But life changed. It took us away from the place we always envisioned for ourselves. We can use these tools we gained, with God, in a different place and see some amazing results! It just takes the faith of these fishermen, and the love that comes naturally from walking with Jesus. I challenge you to consider your gifts, skills, and training and partner them with Jesus. How can you help change lives today?

Mark 1:16-17, Colossians 3:23, Ecclesiastes 9:10

J.O.Y. Life Challenge:

There is no greater task than serving others. Are you volunteering for a cause that is important to you and God's will for your life? If not, your challenge for today is to do some research and sign up for some sort of volunteering opportunity. The time you spend helping others will carry you to places you can't imagine.

Relationally Speaking

Jesus is relational. So are humans. Someone, somewhere helped you find Jesus. Can you remember that "falling in faith" feeling? It's even better than falling in love because it is eternal. Who can you help discover that in your life? What do you need to be brave enough, outgoing enough, challenging enough to share Jesus?

So often we look at evangelism as the job of a pastor or church goer, but truly, that couldn't be further from God's plan. We are all witnesses to Jesus if we call Him our Savior. It's a simple fact. You can't fight it. The way in which you live that truth out is important.

No, you don't have to help people learn about Jesus Christ through a long sermon series or aggressively handing out biblical tracts. But you do need to open your home, your heart and your Bible. Open up to the possibility of sharing your faith with others. Brush up on your prayer life and reboot your Bible reading so that you are ready when the opportunity comes to share your faith.

Mark 16:15, Matthew 9:37-38, 1 Peter 3:15

Dear Jesus, how brave You were! Surely it must have taken so much courage to go out and share the message of salvation when You were looked down upon, ridiculed, and eventually put to death. Lord, I too face difficulty in sharing the message that You began and ended in Your life and death and resurrection. My struggles are more internal, and my fear creeps in when I think about sharing the message of salvation. Help me, Lord. I need to know what to say. I need to know what to pray with others. Give me Your courage and Your words as I go through today and every day! I love you Jesus! I ask for all of this in Your precious name, Amen.

Bologna

There is bologna in this world people. Big old piles of it. And we have to watch out for it, everywhere we go because the enemy longs to stuff us so full of it that we can't move or act because we are sick.

This bologna we are taught culturally about "Never Look Back" or "No Regrets" is ridiculous. We all look back at our lives and wish certain things had been done differently. It's a falsehood to say that we don't, or that we can't. It is healthy and even valuable to see where we have come from in order to be at peace about where we are going.

What have you lived through? Those moments that were agonizing made you stronger. Who has influenced you? Those people were and are crucial to recognize. We must learn about God's vision for our lives through our experiences. He has promised to always hold us in His righteous right hand, no matter where we have been or where we are going.

While I think it is possible to live without shame or fear of condemnation in Christ, I am not sure human beings can live without regrets. Where have you been, my Friend? It has everything to do with where you are going!

Romans 8:1, Isaiah 41:10

J.O.Y. Life Challenge:

What mistakes, regrets or struggles from your life can you hand over to God today? Today's challenge is to find a stone and to write a word on it that describes the burden of regret that is plaguing you. Then, pray. When you arrive at a place in your prayer that you feel comfortable handing the heavy weight to God, do so. Throw the rock out, somewhere you know that you will never see it again, and remember that God has forgiven us through Jesus' precious sacrifice.

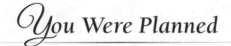

You Were Planned

When I was a girl, I had a fascinating conversation with a boy. He had been telling me that he was very close to his sister; they were best friends. Continuing, he revealed that he believed that before humans were born their spirits hung out in separate cocoons in heaven. His theory was that siblings all inhabited these little cocoons together.

It's a fairly bizarre idea, and there is no wonder why I haven't forgotten it after all this time! However, I think at the heart of his little concept was the desire for confirming that God had intended for everything in our lives to happen before we were even born, i.e. this guy being so close to his sister was part of God's great plan for his life

This kid believed in belonging to his family from pre-conception. Its rather mind blowing, when I think of the fact that while God may not have nestled us into cocoons with our siblings, He certainly knew us, planned for us, and desired for us to walk with Him.

Friend, you have a distinct purpose. You are meant to walk with the Lord, and you can trust that He will never leave you wondering what to do, but will instead guide you with His Holy Spirit. You are meant to share the word of His love with others, and you can trust that every effort you give will be multiplied.

Proverbs 3:5-6, Psalm 9:10, Matthew 5:14-16

Dear God, I want to thank you from the depths of my soul for having a plan for my life for longer than I could ever understand. Please, help me understand these simple truths about my purpose, and to put aside my many plans in order to choose Your will for my life. I love you Lord Jesus! I pray for all of these things in Your mighty name, Jesus. Amen.

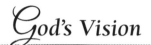

God's Vision

My life is the antithesis of glamorous. I am okay with this, not being an overly girly woman. But the world makes me think that my life should be sparkly and new and flashy; and it always makes me think these thoughts when I am at my lowest.

When there is baby spit up running down my shirt, my hair looks like something a bird wouldn't even nest in, when there are no clothes that fit or look right, and my spirit is equally frayed and tattered; that is when I long for and crave the illicit drug of all women; glamour.

What does this have to do with God's vision for my life or yours? Everything! His vision for our life because His vision stems from His love, which is perfect in that it not only equips us with all that we need to endure the not so glamorous life, but it also clothes us in something mightier even than a little black dress and a great haircut. If you are feeling ugly, unappreciated, unkempt, weak, or rundown, take heart. God loves us and sees our beauty, always.

1 Peter 3:3-4, Song of Solomon 4:7, Proverbs 31:30

J.O.Y. Life Challenge:

If you haven't already figured it out, I love to journal. When I am feeling particularly dowdy, I like to do a writing exercise that I call "Taking a Shower." Write down all the words that you can think of, moments, memories or times in which you felt beautiful, inside and out. Before you have gone a few lines, you should feel the grime of your life beginning to get cleaned out. Let those words and memories carry you through your darkest moments, always knowing God's love for you endures forever.

His vision stems from His love.

Muscle Through

If my life depended on perseverance and self-discipline, I am not sure that a year ago I would have made it. But this year has been different. God has taken my fickle nature and whipped it into shape. Every spiritual muscle that deals with self-discipline has been stretched and pulled, and though I have a lot more to learn, I think the fact that I am still standing after such a learning year proves that I built some muscle mass in the perseverance department!

What has God been teaching you this year, month, week, day, moment? It's important! If He has given you multiple opportunities to learn a lesson, He needs you to be stronger in an area for His will to be done in your life. Sometimes this looks like the same scenario recurring over and over again. Other times it may be different situations but the same issue at the heart of each struggle. I know it hurts. The pain is real and raw and at times fierce. But don't give up, Friend. The Lord will hold you and keep you as you muscle through.

Philippians 3:12-14, Number 6:24-26

God, I am calling out in struggle to You today. These struggles (name your issues) seem impossible to overcome. I do not want to try to escape them any longer. I do not want to give up. I want to muscle through this, Father, because I know You are going to grow in me through this challenge. But I need Your help. Please God, help me to find a way to focus on You, to trust in You, to know that You will bless me and keep me as I go through this storm. Thank you, God. I love you, Lord! For all these things I pray in Your mighty name Jesus. Amen

$\mathcal{L}$iving like Jesus

Have you ever been needed by complete strangers? Many people show up to work each day with the job description of caring for the needs of people that they have never met before! Medical professionals, emergency crews, service workers and more, clock in at their jobs in order to care for other people. Those "other people" are the people we call family, friends, neighbors. You, and I, will also cross paths with so many people that call "belong" to others. With all of these connections we have throughout the day, it can be tough to actively seek kindness and behave in a manner that honors Jesus.

But we must choose to show joy. Light. Kindness. Our actions towards those who may not mean much to us will impact the world, whether we see it or not. How do you want those emergency crews, servers, and customer service reps to treat your loved ones? Be that way today, Friend. It was Jesus' second command, and it's the way to change the world.

Jesus came to serve with love and kindness. He was humble and His glory wasn't fully realized here on earth. Let's be grateful today that these things came to pass, because it is the example of Jesus that leads us to be full of light today.

Matthew 7:12, Matthew 5:14-16

God, You made so many people! How You use us all is beyond my realm of understanding, but I am so grateful that You are God and that You know us all and see our spirits and our needs. Jesus, please overflow into my spirit right now. I need Your perfect light to shine from me as I encounter strangers and loved ones today. Be my guide, as I live in this world and walk among my fellow men. Let me see the people I come across today through Your eyes! And Jesus, thank you for loving me enough to have also walked this walk on earth. I love you Lord! In Jesus' name I pray, Amen.

Jesus came to serve with love and kindness.

Celebrate with J.O.Y.

The first time we try something, do something new, or meet someone, it is impressed upon us for a long time, maybe forever. Jesus turned water to wine as His first public miracle, and while the back story to this is disputed, one thing is for sure: Jesus' mother asked Him to *do* something that would bring joy to a wedding party.

When He turned the water to wine, He was making it clear that He believed in celebration, especially for those who gather to honor each other in matrimony. I think a little foreshadowing to the wedding of the bride of Christ (the church) and His holy self was going on that day. So whether you lift a glass to toast life this week or not, may you have celebration and *joy* in your heart!

Yes, life is hard. Yes, we all struggle with some horrific burdens, but truthfully, there are still blessings in abundance to thank God for. Can you see them? Can you take time today to just praise God, and thank Him, no matter what storm you are walking through?

Psalm 16:11, Psalm 118:24, Psalm 37:4-5

J.O.Y. Life Challenge:

Write down 10 different things to thank God for on sticky notes. Scatter them around today, in places where you will see them as you go about your business. Take little moments to praise the Lord as well, as your find reasons to celebrate the life God has given you!

Guts and Love

The second recorded miracle Jesus performed had a lot to do with the "O" in J.O.Y Life. There was a man, crippled and lame, who had by God's grace, some of the best friends in history. They carried his weak body to a house where Jesus was preaching. When they got there, it was too crowded to get in. So with a little moxie and maverick, the men climbed up onto the roof, cut a hole in it, and lowered their friend down to where Jesus would have no other option but to see their suffering companion.

Jesus, and probably everyone in the house, was aware of the obvious; this guy's friends had guts and love. But their faith and persistence was what Jesus exclaimed over when He did indeed heal the crippled man.

What a party they must have had when they walked with their healed friend out of that crowd! The "Other" people in our lives and how we treat them is highly important to God. Surrounding ourselves with those who can lift us up and those whom we can lift up with our faith walk is going to result in some major miracles. Nothing means more than being prayed for and cared about! Who can you lift up to God today?

Mark 2:4-6, Mark 10:27, Ecclesiastes 4:9-10

Dear Father, You are so full of power and might. How amazing it must have been for the crippled man to have been healed. His friends, too, must have rejoiced in Your mercy and love. Please, dear Father, heal my friend. Take the brokenness in them and make them new. Show mercy on them and their plight. Give ear to their cries. Hear my petition for my loved one. God, I know You are a God of miracles, and today, I am trusting You for the miraculous. I love you Lord, and it is in the mighty name of Jesus that I pray, Amen.

Miraculous Love

While Jesus was in a busy crowd, a woman, so full of faith in His ability to heal her, reached out, and touched His robe. Her expectation was simple; if only she touched a small part of His presence, she would be better. For years she had been plagued with an illness, and it was so bad that those in the community considered her "unclean," which was pretty much the worst state of existence back then.

Sure enough, the small caress of His robe on her fingers, partnered with her unwavering faith, healed her. That's a miracle in itself. But, and that is a holy but, Jesus didn't stop there. He paused in a huge crowd and took His time to find the woman, to speak to her. He wants to acknowledge our faith, friends, beyond just the miracles that happen when we believe.

He wants to be an active part of the life we live once a miracle has occurred. He cares, so deeply for us, no matter what titles the world has given us. His devotion is beyond my comprehension, but make His miracles even more profound, don't you think?

Luke 8:43-47

J.O.Y. Life Challenge:

Miracles are too quickly forgotten. Take a few minutes today to reflect on your life. When did God save you, someone close to you, a stranger? What miracles have you witnessed? There is no way that you haven't ever seen a miracle, I promise! Thank God for these miraculous works today.

He cares, so deeply for us, no matter what titles the world has given us.

God Sees...

One Sunday morning, my husband of almost a decade and I, were at odds. We'd had a leisurely morning and then it was time to get ready for church. We argued over silly things, but our anger escalated quickly, fueled by sleep deprivation and the chaos of life.

We got to church late, cranky, and not united. And wouldn't you know it, our pastor spoke on anger. It may not seem miraculous to you, but knowing that God saw exactly what we were doing and sent a message that applied to our lives seemed like a miracle to me, especially since I had been starved of sermons, unable to attend church for about two months until that morning!

God always sees us, you and me, and if we are listening and looking, we will see Him provide just what we need most, our daily bread, which is a miracle in itself. But what is even more important than paying attention and being aware of God's provision in the mundane and miraculous is our reception and actions in response.

Of course the hubs and I apologized and worked hard to repair the ugly we had made that morning. We sought forgiveness and worked hard to prevent it happening in the future. What door has God been knocking on, trying to get in, in your life? Open that door, and move all the clutter out of the way so He can walk straight to you!

Matthew 6:26, Deuteronomy 29:5, Isaiah 41:10

Dear God,

Help me to move out of Your way, so that You can be free to do miracles in my life. I want to see You at work, and I want to be free to let You be in control. Help me God! Bring light to the dark areas that I have held tight to, and open my eyes to what You are doing. Thank you God, I love you so! In Jesus mighty name I pray, Amen.

$\mathcal{P}$rioritizing Others

J.O.Y Life is about the order of our priorities; by putting Jesus (J), and others (O), in front of yourself(Y), you should have a more meaningful life with greater joy. The biggest reason I started this encouragement was to remind myself and others what Jesus does, and how He came that we might have life and an abundant life at that. I've found that reminder to help keep me on track with a life directed for J.O.Y.

Today, what are some Jesus thoughts you can hold onto? How about the ministry He lived out; the incomprehensible love He exemplified in His perfect life and outreach? Can you mimic His mighty influence today as you reach out into the other people around you?

God is always waiting with His arms wide open, but group hugs are so much more rewarding. Let's take our friends, neighbors, co-workers, and even enemies into His arms with us today.

Acts:13:47, Romans 1:16, Acts 20:24

J.O.Y. Life Challenge:

Make a list of all the people in your life today that you can reach out to. No need to make it an insurmountable task! Pray over the list and ask God to give you three or four people, and do so with great courage and love, just like Jesus!

God is always waiting with His arms wide open, but group hugs are so much more rewarding.

God's Faithfulness through Miracles

In 2011, my husband walked from the coast of Oregon to the North Carolina coast in order to raise funds for a charity. I went with him, toting our 18-month-old baby. I didn't do all the walking, but I was never far from my husband in case he needed back-up. One beautiful day in the crispy fall, I put my son in a back-pack carrier and we went hiking. It was no different than many days we had spent on the road. We made it to the top of a crest, and I headed to the edge to peer down at the large body of water below.

Somehow, my son's carrier got caught in a tree limb as I gazed down; so when I attempted to turn around I was stuck. Worse, the branch seemed determined to push us over the edge of the cliff. Truthfully, I thought we were going to die. I pushed so hard against that branch's force that I found my back screaming in pain. Every muscle in my body worked together to survive, and fear quickly seeped into my heart. I called for help, but no human assistance came. Adrenaline, surging through my veins at the speed of Olympic racers, roared in my ears.

My spirit remembered to call out to God, when it seemed most dark for us. Suddenly, my son began to scream, and something happened, loosening us to safety. The release of the branch was the last scary moment, the force of it almost too great for me to resist as it tried one last time to push us over the edge. I nearly collapsed when we made our distance from the edge of the cliff. My entire body shook, and I sat holding my little boy, whose cheek was freshly gashed from the battle with the killer branch. My life was so precious to me in that moment, and I have no words for the emotions I held in my heart for my son's.

I had never been that grateful to be alive. I've never understood how we got tangled up, but had it not been for God, and His miracles, I am certain I wouldn't be typing this now. He is always there; this was reinforced deeply into my heart that day. I am praying God shows you His faithfulness through miracles this day and beyond. Hold tight to those memories of His miraculous nature, because we forget so easily!

Luke 1:37, Matthew 19:26, Matthew 21:21

Miraculous Father, thank You for Your incredible strength that has always been an umbrella over me through life's downpours. Please, show me miracles today, and through this week and month and my whole life, that will remind me of Your power over humanity, the universe and all. I praise You for Your unfathomable depth and strength. I love you Lord, and I pray for all of this in the mighty name of Jesus! Amen

Quiet Miracles

She was so young. And afraid. And beautiful. And pregnant. She sat in my office, and after two meetings was still determined to abort her child. I accompanied her to an ultrasound. I saw in her eyes all the fear, stubbornness and determination I had seen all along. I felt uneasy, and told a colleague that this unborn child was a lost life from where I sat. I was at peace with my role in her life and the encouragement I had given, but sad, so sad that night. I didn't hear from her, though I checked in routinely. Two months later we got a call. It turns out she decided to keep the child, which she had just discovered was a little girl! I met her for lunch to celebrate, and saw her fear still there, but her excitement as well. She shared her child's name, a sure sign that this child was already loved and adored. It was a miracle for me, because I was so sure she had made up her mind differently. I love how God, given time and our surrender, can perform amazing miracles!

God's miracles are funny in that they can come in grand scale packages, all at once, like a waterfall deluge. Or they can sneak in, under the radar as quick as a wink, leaving the recipient scratching his or her head wondering what happened. Jesus performed both types of miracles; water into wine, healing the sick, and raising the dead back to life were some of the big things. But He also walked among us flawless, never being conned into sin, which looks like a small thing in comparison, but can arguably be the biggest miracle of all.

This young lady said the one thing that changed her mind on the decision to keep her child was a devotional she had been given. Not the ultrasounds she had seen of her child's heartbeat. Not the people in her life. A little book, seemingly insignificant, was used for God's great and amazing purpose! Look out for the small, quiet miracles today, because the power they hold to change your life is great!

Luke 9:16-17, John 3:16

Holy God, Thank You for coming to the earth in humility. The miracle of Your life is a forgotten treasure so much of the year, but I pray that today I would remember the miracle of Christmas. Use this story to guide me to open my eyes to my own life and see the small miracles You have in store for me right here! Thank you God, for Your provision, Your forgiveness, Your strength and power! You are awesome and I praise Your name for the breath You have given me this day. For all these things I pray in Jesus name. Amen

*Look out for the small, quiet
miracles today, because
the power they hold to
change your life is great!*

*B*attle Ready

Have you ever noticed that the moment you set out to accomplish something important for your spiritual growth, you get sick, or an unexpected bill shows up, or a close relation wounds you? There is an active enemy to our spiritual growth, and He lies in wait for moments such as this to destroy our resolve, kill our drive to draw near God, and we don't even notice many times.

Today, let's take an offensive role in our own spiritual lives. Let's see the spiritual battle around us. Where are you struggling? What is this struggle keeping you from handing over to God? Is it crushing your desire to love others? Love yourself or your life? Understanding that our enemy has only one goal, and that is our destruction, should help us to blow the dust off of our old armor and strap it on!

But remember, we are not ever alone. God is with us always. He sent His own son as our champion, to fight for us and to lead us through this battle with a fierce and mighty strength. Rely on God for your power to battle; seek Jesus for His source of power today!

John 10:10, Ephesians 6:10-18

Mighty God, Please see me in my battle today! Send Jesus, to lift this burden from my shoulders. Send me fellow warriors to align myself with to fight this enemy, and remind me that we have already won the war! Jesus, show me Your light and guiding strength, and speak to me through my armor as I place it on my body! You are great and mighty, and worthy of all my praise, Jesus! I pray for all of this in Your name. Amen.

Miracles in the Everyday

When I sit down to consider miracles, I start at the beginning of my life. I go all the way back to that point so that I can look at the years one by one and consider what miracles I saw and was a part of. The first miracle I encountered, one that I thank God for every day, is the miracle of my existence. In the 1980's abortion peaked at an all-time high, with teen pregnancy soaring and being one of the leading causes of this spike. Statistically, I should have joined the approximately 59 million that have been aborted in America to date. But God doesn't look at people statistically. We are all individuals. And I thank God every day that life is miraculous, and He blessed me with parents who, though young and wild and free, valued life.

As I continue to peruse my life in these quiet moments, I realize all that has happened to me, every miracle, God has used for the purposes of His plan. Maybe your life didn't start with similar circumstances as mine, but all life is sacred, and a miracle to behold. The very breath we breathe has purpose and God wants to use it in His kingdom to bring love and joy to the world. You have seen the miraculous, whether you recall it instantly or not. God is here, and always has been, Friend.

Psalm 77:14, Psalm 86:12

J.O.Y. Life Challenge:

Take time today to peruse your memories of your life. What miracles have you been a part of? Thank God for each moment He has given you a miraculous outcome, and hold onto those moments as you combat the difficulties of today!

The very breath we breathe has purpose.

$\mathcal{H}$e is Greatest

I am constantly humbled by the fact that it is God's love, and not our deeds, that get us to heaven. I also have been amazed to find God right there jumping out at me with miracles, big huge ones, right after I feel like I have done something important. It's as if He wants to remind me that no matter what, He is bigger than me-and this is good!

It's good because I can get "big-head syndrome" and think I am this wonderful do-gooder. Guys, miracles are the remedy to big head syndrome. Miracles are impossible, but for God.

A few weeks after I gave birth to one of my children, one of my closest friends was hit at interstate speeds by a tractor trailer. Her car bashed between the truck and the guard rail like a pin ball six times. The vehicle was totaled, and when she emerged, she was almost completely unscathed.

Here I was thinking I was big stuff for incubating and carrying a baby to term and birth almost without any help (because let's be honest, moms do all the pregnancy work on their own!) And while it's okay to be proud of our accomplishments, and trust me, pregnancy and birth is a big accomplishment, there were many moments when I was pulling my pride and stretching it to epic proportions. There was God, with a big ol' wake up call that sounded something like this to me:

"Honey, you couldn't have carried life without me. And you certainly can't protect it like I can. Let me have credit for the miracle of life, of the strength I give mothers, of the power you felt when you conquered delivery of that sweet baby."

God has miraculously come to the aid of His people, countless times and in so many ways. While humans are remarkable, you included, we must stand today and acknowledge that the creator of life, of miracles, is God in heaven.

Mark 10:27, Jeremiah 32:27, Psalm 139:13-14

Dear God,

Please forgive me for my pride and lack of humility. Help me to see myself the way You see me today. Help me to understand the strength that You want to offer; that I might be able to step away from the strength I have been depending on in myself. Thank you for miracles! Show me Your miraculous works in action today, please! I love you, Lord. For all of this I pray in Jesus miraculous name. Amen.

What's in a Name?

Throughout my third pregnancy, my husband and I bickered and discussed what to name our little boy. We wanted a name he could wear his whole life long: a name to pronounce his individual strength and confidence every day.

A name is important, because it gives identity in this huge world. We have a vision for our son's life; not the details so much as the overall goal. We hope to see him grow in strength, wisdom and love for the Lord. We believe that his name has a lot to do with that plan.

The name we chose means "more son, carrier of Christ," because we were excited to have another son to carry Christ in this world! God has a special name for us as well; He told Simon he was now "Peter: the rock on which the church was built." Jacob became "Israel" and Abraham also started life with a different moniker.

We may not hear God's special name for us until we get to heaven, but trust that God has a unique name and vision for you and it's worth leaping recklessly into His arms in pursuit of hearing it.

John 1:42, Isaiah 43:1

J.O.Y. Life Challenge:

What names are you called? Are there any ugly names, old, painful monikers that have scarred you? Denounce them. Refuse them. Write them down, and then destroy them. Wad them up, stomp on them, and throw them out.

Decide today that you are chosen, precious and realize that God has called you by name. And His name for you is beautiful because He knows that you are beautiful.

Trust that God has a unique name and vision for you and it's worth leaping recklessly into His arms in pursuit of hearing it.

About the Author

Angel Hinman is a sleep deprived mother of three wild things
and wife to an amazing husband. She lives on a small farm with
her crew in the foothills of North Carolina, where she spends
her time worshipping Jesus, homeschooling, attempting to learn
Chinese, teaching art classes, climbing trees and managing J.O.Y.
Life. Angel has also authored Water Walk America, a detailed
account of her husband's journey by foot across America.

For more information, visit facebook.com/LivetheJOYLife
instagram@LifetheJOYLife

Printed in the United States
By Bookmasters